MW00442889

# YOU'RE GONNA DIE SOON

## The Key to Unlocking Happiness and Success

### JOSH DRIVER

YOU'RE GONNA DIE SOON

THE KEY TO UNLOCKING HAPPINESS AND SUCCESS

Josh Driver

ISBN (Print Edition): 978-1-66785-579-0

ISBN (eBook Edition): 978-1-66785-580-6

# CONTENTS

# INTRODUCTION

Hello! I appreciate you taking time to read this book. Soon, I hope, you will appreciate me for writing it. The human mind is the most powerful tool in the world. How you perceive and respond to events, and how you train and shape your mind, will ultimately determine the outcome of your life… for better or for worse. The power is in your hands. So, don't waste it.

In this book, you will learn things that "experts" took years to understand and what some people will, unfortunately, never know. The great news is you may not agree with everything in this book, and that's okay. That's normal. I strongly believe that this book can and will improve your life. Some lives may change just a little bit, and for some it may be earth-shattering, like it was for me. What you enjoy in this book, feel free to share with your family and friends. We all need good directions in our lives. I truly believe that we all can learn something from this book, and that it can change lives for the better. You may find yourself gaining a whole new perspective, or simply receiving a reminder to help you in your business and personal life.

This world is full of people force feeding you their "ideas" and what they think the "best" course of action is. Truth is, there is a different formula for everyone. You can make it your own.

My way, thoughts, and ideas may not be the very best. However, if you learn just a little bit, that will make reading this book more than worth it. No one person knows everything, and no one is perfect, so you can decide what works best for you. We only get one go-around on the carousel that is life. So, live life like you mean it. Don't waste it being unhappy and unfulfilled, and learn how to react. With the right response, you can create the best path forward in the battle for happiness and success.

And that is where our journey begins...

# CHAPTER 1:

# YOU'RE GONNA DIE

My dad had me late in life, at about 50 years old. During his last few years, he would get serious about once a month. He would start saying that he wasn't going to be around for very long. He wanted me to remember everything he taught me. So, Dad – acting like he was higher than giraffe's nuts – would go into these long, drawn out speeches, as if accepting an Oscar. I usually listened, until one night I'd had enough. I got mad and told him to stop bringing this negative *death talk* into the universe.

But that was when he said it: "Son, you're going to die soon."

It hit me strangely, considering the fact that I was 25 years old. Here I was, thinking that I had a nice long life ahead of me. I was about to find out that it wasn't really about how much time we have left, but what we do with that time.

I didn't really understand it fully until I sat down to write this book. It was then that I learned what I needed to focus on. Now that I've grown, I truly understand what my father meant. We're *all* gonna die too soon. And so many of us live in an unhappy place – we just need a little help.

Something Confucius said really sums it all up: "We have two lives, and the second begins when we realize we only have one."

We tend to spend so much of our time worried, fearful, anxious, and pissed off about everything. We get frustrated about things that are insignificant, and focus on stuff that doesn't matter. Now, life will never be easy, but it wasn't supposed to be. Completely changing the way you think is hard. I, personally, am far from an expert. However, if you start to change your thinking about one thing at a time, this book will help you. It will change both your every day and your future. Because face it…

You're gonna die soon.

That might be pretty obvious – the fact that all of us will die soon. When that is, only God knows. Whether you're 18 or your 80, *soon* is different for everyone. Even if you are 100 years from leaving this crazy beautiful life, that is still too soon. We never have enough time. Plus, we spend most of our lives on negative thoughts, emotions, and actions that eat up that precious time. That's not a negative thought, though. It's a positive thought. Because as soon as you realize this, you will stop spending too much time on the wrong things, being around the wrong people, and having useless thoughts. You will stop being unhappy just *because*.

# CHAPTER 2:

# THIS TOO SHALL PASS

One of the best things about life, and sometimes one of the worst things about life, is that nothing lasts forever. If you're feeling happy – the happiest you've ever been – it will feel like no one can hold a candle to your happiness. I'm sorry to tell you, though, that this will pass. But if you're feeling mad, or sad, or frustrated about the fact that your happiness will pass… that too shall pass. If you're feeling mad, or sad, or frustrated about any-thing – that will pass. So, one of the most important things that you can do is cherish the happy moments while you're in them, and know that sad moments are short-lived.

As humans, we can get trapped in either one of these spaces, which allows them to get the best of us. In the long run, though, there's probably nothing special about how you feel in one spe-cific moment. I can guarantee that it's all been done before. One of the most important keys to get through the rollercoaster of life lies in finding peace in whatever stage you're in.

This peace can be measured if you're working at your cur-rent job. I will give you a personal example. For many years, I was in person-to-person sales. I can safely say it was one of the most difficult sales jobs there is. This wasn't because the product we were selling wasn't good, though. In fact. the product was basically vacations, and who doesn't want a nice vacation? The challenge resided in getting someone to make a decision worth tens of thousands of dollars on that same day you were talking to them. It wasn't the easiest because, as you may know, if someone doesn't make a decision that day, the chances of them actually buying something drops significantly. So, there was definitely stress in this job.

However, some of the very best salespeople understood that some days were good and some days were bad. Fortunately, I did well at my job. I understood people, and I knew how to train my mind.

At this job, the worst that could happen to a new representative was that they could come in and do extremely well for the first month or two. They might be good at their job, but it was often due to luck. Even if they were a naturally great salesperson, that too would pass. I'd seen so many new people get complacent in their happiness, thinking that everything was easy. However, when that tide would start to shift, and the time to get tough arrived, they would always think that they did something completely wrong. This challenge made them think it would be near impossible for them to ever regain what they once had.

One of the best ways to think about life and your day to day is to remember that everything happens in seasons. Sometimes, seasons last longer than they're supposed to. We've all experienced that hot day in September or October after we've put away all our summer clothes. But guess what? If you're waiting on winter while it's summer, there's a pretty good chance winter will arrive eventually. That's right, *Game of Thrones* fans… winter is coming. In fact, I've known many people who have had bad days, and bad days that lasted for more than a couple of days. So, when someone says, "I'm having a bad day," that does not necessarily mean they're having a bad life.

We tend to get ahead of ourselves and let good *todays* get spoiled by bad *yesterdays*. The key (or one of the keys) to life is to never let something in the past ruin a good day – especially when it's something that's out of your control. Regardless of where you are in your life, and whatever you're experiencing, I guarantee you that it will pass. Sometimes, it will be hard to bear. It might feel *impossible* to bear. But you will get through it. Sure, you might be thinking, "That's easier said than done." It probably is. But it's all about tricking your brain into doing what you want it to do.

You might be sitting there reading this book feeling juiced and excited. You might be excited that you can finally be in control! Well, this too shall pass. At some point in the next few days, some kid at school is gonna spit on your lunch (metaphorically speaking... I hope). It's important to keep reminding yourself that it will pass. And I mean that – keep reminding yourself. Just hearing it once isn't going to work. Tell yourself every day that life is short. Remind yourself that you're always going to be in different types of moods. Find happiness in every mood – regardless of the situation you're in. Because it *will* pass.

# CHAPTER 3:

## HAPPINESS IS
## YOUR DECISION

I've often said that the only difference between a homeless person and a billionaire is billions of dollars. A homeless person can be just as happy as someone with billions of dollars. Why? Because it is all a mindset, though not in the way you may think. It's not that the rich person is more intelligent, or better off than the other. In fact, the homeless person may actually be the happiest of the two. A homeless person might be happier than anyone you've ever met, even after roaming the cold streets and begging for change to buy a hot dog from the 7-Eleven. They might even be happier than that billionaire with a mansion and seven cars.

Happiness is ultimately up to the beholder. Many people who have everything are more miserable than the people who have nothing. Our *things* don't truly bring us prolonged happiness – these items keep us wanting more. True happiness, though, leads us down a deep hole of understanding. When you finally find that happiness, you achieve emotional control, allowing you to be happy anywhere and anytime.

I know at this point, your eyes may have glazed over. You may even be shaking your head in anger and disbelief. You might even be thinking, "Well, Josh, if I had one billion dollars, I guarantee I would be happier!"

I agree, you probably would be happy for a while. So would I! That is not really in question. The question is: do you truly know where your happiness comes from?

To set the mood, let me be clear – I'm not a person who believes that money is bad or that rich people are bad. In fact, I've yet to see someone frowning on a jet ski. I believe that everybody deserves what they have earned and worked for, and also that money is an invaluable resource. It can help out a lot of people, and ultimately give you and your family a great life. Don't misunderstand the point. I have been happy with a bunch of money, and I've been happy with no money.

The point is not that you should stop craving expensive things or experiences. I'm human, I know I do. It's okay to want nice things. The truth I want you to remember – before you get your underwear in a twist – is that it all starts with you. How you feel in the moment (whether swamped at your job, or sitting on a beach with your smokin' hot lover and a cold drink in your hand) is what matters. The point is to have emotional control and restraint. Happiness is part of the journey. It's not just the top of the mountain, or a dot on a map. It's a path you must choose, or a road you must follow. It is not just be your final destination.

Because remember: you're gonna die soon. You don't know when that end point will be. Might as well enjoy what you're experiencing *now*.

We're all predisposed to think we're *supposed to* be happy. For most of us its in our culture and starts when we are children.

I was in third grade when I first felt the sting of Cupid's arrow. It came in the form of a crumpled up piece of notebook paper, probably because it was inside Michelle's pocket for too long. She had practically thrown it at me right before class was over, giving me no time to say anything or catch up to her as she ran inside her mom's minivan.

It went something like this:

*Dear Josh,*
*You're a really cool guy and you remind me of a teddy bear*
*and I like you a lot, will you hang out with me?*
*♡ Michelle*

When I left school, I felt something I'd never felt before. It was a high like none other. I was ready to take on the world.

I walked into class the next day with the biggest smile on my face. My chest was pumped up as I entered my castle. I was ready to rescue my princess from the dragon… or maybe just sit with her at lunch.

I talked to Michelle on the playground, where she admitted that everything in the note was true. She did have feelings for me. Of course, we were in third grade, so who knows what that even meant. Whatever its true meaning, though, it was real. I just knew I was the happiest I had ever been.

For the next week, we hung out as much as we could. We shared laughs and sat together any chance we got.

But the next week, something changed. Michelle was becoming distant. You could say I was quite intuitive for a third grader. I had to address this rift in our relationship. So, I went up to her at recess. I asked her what was going on. Why was she being so distant?

She looked down at her feet. It took her a few seconds, then she said it: "I don't feel that way about you anymore."

Saying that it felt like someone had punched me in the stomach 227 times before an airbag deployed in my face would be an understatement. My world was over. The bliss I'd felt for the past few days shattered by eight dreadful words.

Okay, yes, we were in third freaking grade! Yes, that was only three grades past kindergarten. I had only just added a second digit to my age. Still, I was sure my life was over, ruined just because some girl said she didn't like me anymore. It had only been a week, at best, but it had been the best week of my life.

Did I mention we were in third grade?

By that point, I had seen more Disney films that Walt himself. I thought my life was one big fairytale because no one had told me anything different. I had heard my mom blare the band Air Supply from the speakers of her Ford Expedition every day. I – like everyone who isn't told that bad things happen, that it's okay to feel sad, and that it will be okay if another third grader breaks your heart – was not prepared for this.

I had been taught from a very young age that grade school would be fantastic. I expected to meet all these new friends, and even get a girlfriend that would invite me to her birthday party. I was going to be the coolest kid in the class.

But think about it – if everyone was the coolest kid in class, there would be no "coolest kid." If everyone had an extraordinary talent, then no one would have an extraordinary talent.

The world is full of heartbreak. In fact, you'll probably get your heart broken around every corner you turn. I just hope that the next time it happens, you're ready for it. Don't look heartbreak in the face and ask, "Why me?" Look it dead in the eyes and say, "Try me!"

Knowing how to face heartbreak will help you embrace happiness when it comes your way.

If being happy for you means sitting on the beach, do it! Keep in mind, though, that you won't be able to do that if you have no cash flow or any money saved.

"Wait, wait, Josh, now you're just contradicting your whole point!"

Wrong! The point is that in order to be where you want to be, and do the things that most of us want to do (80% of which requires money), then yes, you will need money. Barely surviving is not good enough for most people, nor should it be.

You're not going to get money if you don't have a steady mindset. At the same time you cannot miss out on all the small things. To be successful, you'll still have to enjoy the journey. So, be happy while you're working. *That* is how to yield success.

You have choices every morning you wake up. You'll decide what to eat for breakfast, if you're going to brush your teeth or not, and a whether to sit in bed or run around the block. The simple fact is that it is your decision. How you are and how you feel is ultimately up to you. Yes, you can have things and people that give you pleasure. But whether you live in a $100 million mansion or on the street, how you feel about your day and how you feel at your current state is your decision.

Now you may be yelling at this, "Josh, that's just a stupid comparison. Of course, a billionaire is going to feel much better. They have no worries, no real problems."

But that's not always the case. We as humans create problems for ourselves every day, even when there are none. We over-think and over-analyze everything to a fault. We also compare ourselves to others. It is 100% fine to want to see changes in your life – I know I do. We all want new purchases. The point is to remember that it's not the things that are making you happy, it's the happiness that is making you happy. So, make your choices accordingly.

Okay, let's try this. I want you to stop what you're doing for one minute and think about one or two of the happiest times of your life. If you're not driving a motorized vehicle or operating heavy machinery, I also want you to close your eyes. Now I want you to replay this happy memory in your head.

Chances are you have a smile or at least a small grin on your face. The reason for this is that you went to a special place that we all have in your minds. That's where happiness resides. If you're saying to this book, "Well, Josh, that did not work for me," then I guess you're crazy. Just kidding, it just means we need to work on the power of your thoughts. Maybe you were distracted, and that's okay too. Whether you could or couldn't get to that place in your mind, I'm glad you're here. Truth is, none of this is easy and it will take effort and work.

Happiness can be crippled even when we are in a good mood. The minute we doubt ourselves or where our life is going, or think that we're not good enough, we get surrounded. We are swarmed by loud opinions, movies, and friends, then that swarm is regurgitated all over social media:

"Be the best you!!"

"Be better!"

It's as if you're not "there" yet.

Let's face it, most everybody looks happier than you when you're stuck doing work. They also always happen to be on vacation while you are stuck in the office with a three-foot-tall stack of paper on your desk as rain pounds against the window. Your social media shows images of sunshine and daytime cocktails while your boss calls you into their office every five minutes to scream about something frivolous. Okay, I'm exaggerating, but I think you get the point.

The fact is, there is a time and a place for your feelings and thoughts. Not everybody is going to be at the same emotional place as you. If they were, that place would probably get a little bit crowded. We are humans, and humans are weird, but you have more power than you think. So, put that power to work.

# CHAPTER 4:

## DESTINATION ADDICTION

*"Beware of destination addiction, a preoccupation with the idea that happiness is in the next place, the next job, and with the next partner. Until you give up the idea that happiness is somewhere else, it will never be where you are."*

– Robert Holden

When we think of addiction, we don't always think about it in terms of destination. But anything can be an addiction. Anything can get in the way of our way of life and our well-being. This hunt for a destination can be a huge barrier in people's search for happiness and what they believe is the "perfect life." It is natural and often common for some of us to believe that where we are is not where we should be. It doesn't help when everything and everyone around you – your boss, the motivational posters on the wall, and even birthday cards – are telling you to be smarter, be healthier, be sexier, and reach for the stars. You've been told to chase the rainbow, and according to every Skittles commercial, you can even taste the rainbow.

I mean, come on! Really?

As I'm sure you know, much of the communication we experience in our world is part of one big marketing tactic. Someone is always trying to sell you something. As someone who has been in all different areas of sales, I know this for fact. It's not necessarily a bad thing, but it is something you should be aware of.

The people who face adverse effects from destination addiction believe that success is a point on a map. They believe that they will never truly be happy until they reach some kind of pillar, or ultimate goal. To make matters worse, most humans don't know how to set goals, so their goals are never obtainable. Without proper goals, it leaves them grasping for straws. It leaves people feeling incomplete.

Your brain, for the most part, is always moving. Though it doesn't leave your skull (if you're lucky), it is constantly on the go. It will always be several steps ahead of you – whether that's in minutes, month, or even years. That's why you need to make sure you're communicating with your brain. Tell your brain that you are exactly where you want to be. Remind yourself that you are in the moment you were meant for – which is *right now*. You will continue to do the little things today, and eventually you'll reach whatever destination you are supposed to reach tomorrow.

I'm not telling you to completely blow off work, or not go to school, or not be a parent to your child. You still have responsibilities that you must attend to in order to keep your life moving. But I am telling you to reorganize your thoughts.

If you have destination addiction, then you're always on the hunt for some kind of inner peace. But after searching for so long, you'll probably realize that you don't even know what in the hell that means. Don't worry. There's a way to deal with this addiction. The first step would be to say to yourself, "It is okay to be where I am. It is okay to feel how I feel, even if I don't feel perfect. It is even okay if I have a little bit of anxiety – we all do in some form."

This might shock you, so I recommend that the faint of heart sit down. The bottom line is this: no one – not the weather reporter, not the tarot card reader, and not your pastor – knows what the future holds. Guess what? There's only one thing for certain. It's that you are going to die sooner than you want to. So, stop bitching, moaning, and complaining about a destination that is not guaranteed to you. If being rich and living a life of luxury was so easy, then everyone would live in a mansion and drive three different Ferraris.

About ten years before I wrote this book, I was just starting a new job in sales. I moved to Nashville, Tennessee after living in Memphis for a few years. At the time, Nashville was a quickly-growing city, and was starting to become a much more popular tourist spot. Of course, it's always been a huge spot within the music scene, and has also boasted great food and rich southern history. The 2010s was when its popularity really exploded. Many of the people I grew up with came to town because they wanted to visit the city – and of course, hang out with me.

Despite my friends loving the city I lived in, I still didn't feel totally satisfied. I had it in my head that I was not going to be happy until I had $100,000 cash in the bank. Where in the hell that number came from, I have no idea. It was just a nice, round number that sounded good at the time. So, I decided that I was going to work on my off days and stretch myself pretty thin. I had friends coming to town, and though I said I was going to hang out with them, I was working until 9pm and never wanted to hang out afterward. I spent the back half of my 20s avoiding people when they came to town. My only real friend at the time was the "destination" that I had created in my head. I was focusing on something that didn't exist, rather than the very real friends who wanted to hang out with me.

Now, some of you might say, "That's pretty ambitious of you, Josh! Good for you for being a hell of a worker." Sure, I won't tell you that being a hard worker is a bad thing. But you can be a hard worker and still be a good friend. I could have at least tried to see my friends when they were in town. However, I was so dissatisfied with myself that I didn't want to see anyone until I reached my goal of $100,000 in happiness. But what's the point of a hundred thousand dollars if you have zero friends in your life?

There I was, a bachelor in one of the country's hottest cities. I could have been having the time of my life, and yet I wasn't. I wasn't actually happy, I was chasing *after* happiness – a happiness I had tied to a specific amount of money. Eventually, my friends just stopped talking to me altogether, and another passed away. I was losing the chance to be with the people I cared about left and right.

Now, I'm definitely a person who believes that you should work hard for what you believe in. You should work hard for your goals. In fact, I preach that every day. However, I also believe that you should never deny your happiness in your current moment. If you're not satisfied with where you are, you won't truly be happy. I may have been 26 years old, making $13,000 a month with few bills to pay, and still, I was unhappy. I was unsatisfied with who I was, and where I was in life.

I had become inflicted with destination addiction, and in the process, had started to ignore the real things in my life that I passed by.

No destination is guaranteed, but the journey is. So, enjoy the journey, not the place you are trying to reach.

# CHAPTER 5:

## LIFE IS NOT FAIR

Since many of us were kids, we were taught to share with other people… especially when it came to our most prized possessions: our beloved toys. I can't tell you how many times I wanted to rub sand in my friend Johnny's face after he kept snatching my yellow backhoe from my hands just because his mom had told him it was "fair to share."

I never *actually* rubbed sand in his face because I had pretty good manners for a five-year-old (thanks Mom). But the unfairness with the backhoe morphed as I got older. A few years later, it became about how Johnny was allowed to stay out later than I could. *My* mom wouldn't let me stay out past 5:00pm, but Johnny's mom let him stay out until 6:30. That was a whole hour and a half longer than me! There was so much within that time that I never got to experience! How many adventures had I missed out on after being stuck at home during those evening hours? That was super unfair to me. I was not having it. But I can still hear my mother's country twang whenever I would complain: "Well, Joshua, life is just not fair."

This upset me to my inner core. Of course, at that time I viewed it as something being kept from me. It was a conspiracy against me, Josh. I was being robbed. I was a victim of a crime, of the worst kind of injustice. I was somehow held back, or in some kind of prison because of that lack of fairness we hear so much about. I'd thought that things were supposed to be fair. I, like many of us, was not prepared for what the world had in store for me. Finding out that the world wasn't fair was like watching the rocket ship that was my life exploding in midair. I learned that in reality, the world was one big competition. In fact, my world ended up being the opposite of fair. There is always a bigger fish, and it's always on someone else's hook. There's always going to be somebody smarter, better, richer, or further along than you. Some people may even get to stay an hour and half later than you! Some people may be luckier, and some people just may work harder, but you may never see that. You will just think it's unfair.

I had a grade school teacher who used to say, "If 'fair' only comes once a year, it has more cotton candy than your current situation..." I remember everyone in my class getting so irritated whenever Mr. Thomas would say this. Truth was, though, he was just trying to get us ready for the real world.

When you view the world from such a young age, your perception of what is fair and unfair is totally off-balance. Life really never has been and never will be what we perceive as fair. As soon as you realize that life is never going to be fair, you will finally be able to get past the disenchantment and self-pity. Some people throw around the word "fair" like it's a bunch of hot dogs at a major league baseball game. Some people use it as a crutch. It's a crippling excuse for mediocrity. They use it as a reason as to why they don't have the skills or abilities that other people have. They want to be good at something, whether that's in sports, school, business, or even in drawing pictures of cats. Whatever the hell they want to be good at, the fact of the matter is that it's not about what's fair or about what's unfair. It's about who's going to put in the time and effort – even if you don't always see that. Because that's the real way to get good at something.

At times, you might find yourself saying, "Well, they're just able to do that because they are friends with the boss," or, "They're the teachers favorite, of course they got an A," or "Their great great grandfather was Picasso, no wonder they're so good at doodling." We make up all kinds of reasons why someone else is good at something that we struggle with. As I said, the mind is a powerful thing. You can trick yourself into believing anything you want. Saying that things aren't fair is acting like a victim. By blaming the unbalanced, cosmic scales, you imply that the universe itself has something against you. But being a victim is not the way to success. Victims are not happy, and victims don't accomplish great things for themselves.

Of course, there are times when there is a finger on the scale at the expensive of others. That's not just about life being unfair – that's discrimination. Once again, what's important is how we use the term. Me not being able to stay out past 5:00pm was obviously not discrimination. *Fairness* has nothing to do with men and women being paid the same amount for the same job, or ensuring that people of all races be given the same job opportunities. Those are about human decency – about not discriminating.

So don't start saying, "Josh, things have to be fair!" I get it. If you have the ability to do good, then you should take that opportunity. Saying that "Life isn't fair" is not an excuse to hurt others, or block them from opportunity. There's a difference between acknowledging the fact that there's a big mountain that we all have to climb and actively pushing boulders down that mountain to block specific people. There's a difference between saying that everyone has to climb and actually knocking people back down to the bottom. The key is in recognizing what you can and can't control.

Sometimes, what we can't control comes in the form of experiences. If you're anything like me, you have not yet mastered the art of splitting your existence to be in more than one place at a time. That's where *FOMO* comes in.

FO·MO.

Ah, yes the "fear of missing out." It means different things for different people, but when I looked it up in the Oxford dictionary, I found:

*FOMO – noun (INFORMAL)*
*1. anxiety that an exciting or interesting event may currently be happening elsewhere, often aroused by posts seen on social media.*

Honestly, this kind of concerns me. When I think about the fear of missing out that I felt when I was growing up, it was usually because my friends were all together at someone else's house. It was that itchy feeling I got at the back of my head because I wasn't there. I couldn't help but wonder what they were talking about. Were they playing the coolest new videogame, or taking a brand new toy out of a box? What inside jokes were they making without me? It's sort of the same thing now, but unfortunately, the prevalence of social media has catapulted it to brand new levels. It's not just your mind wondering what might be happening without you, because now you have pictures to prove it – evidence of a fun time that you are not a part of.

Social media messes with our brains, giving us emotional whiplash as we scroll or tap from post to post. We don't know if we're happy or sad. One second we're enjoying cute cat pictures, but the next second we are clobbered with all of jealousy-inducing pictures. We see people on vacation *supposedly* enjoying their lives:

*Hey loves! I'm here on this beautiful tropical island where bad feelings are not allowed! And look! My cat got his hair braided!*

Meanwhile, you're stuck selling more of the same stuff at work. Your email inbox is overflowing (which you didn't even know was possible). The only break you get is scrolling through social media, where you keep being reminded of the fact that you are *not* on a tropical island.

I'm sorry to say, your life will not always be perfect. Your life will not always be luxurious. Your life will probably not always be happy. There's also a great chance that you won't live on a luxurious island inside a $20 million mansion with the helicopter pad on top. Statistically, you won't even own a $10 million dollar mansion. But guess what? That's okay.

Your current life – whatever you're doing, wherever you are, and whoever you're with – is the only thing you have right now. Ultimately, you choose to feel however you want to feel in the precious moments that are given to you. You can feel like you are missing out, or you can choose to live in what's real. Dream of being somewhere else, or be in the moments you already have. Choose wisely.

It's possible to move beyond this condition called FOMO, and I'm proof of that. For the majority of my life – mainly my teenage and college years – I suffered from FOMO pretty bad. I was close to my family growing up, I decided to go to a college that was only thirty miles from home. It was nice not be too far away from where I grew up, but I still felt the FOMO sting. My friends did not feel that close. I couldn't handle knowing that my high school buddies were spending so much time without me. What adventures were they going on without me? What experiences were they enjoying without their old pal Josh?

It was such a maddening experience. Part of me wanted my friends to no longer have any fun. I wanted them to just sit around and do nothing without me there. That would have made me feel better.

I realized that one way to make me feel less sad about missing out with my friends was to make new experiences of my own. So I did that. I made new friends, and created new experiences. I learned that I didn't have to feel upset anymore. I could only be in one place.

And then I wondered how my old high school friends would feel about me making new memories. Maybe *they* felt left out at the thought of me spending time with my new friends.

FOMO is real, but there are billions of experiences happening at any one instance, and you can only experience one of them. How many people out there wish that *they* could experience what *you* are going through?

Don't worry about missing out. If you spend too much time worrying about what you are *not* experiencing, you won't be able to experience what you *are* experiencing.

# CHAPTER 6:

# LIVING IN THE MOMENT

Life has a funny way moving both fast and slow at the same time. If only we could control the speed – speed up the hours you have to spend time at work, and slow down the relaxing moments by the pool. Even though there have been many films and books about it, time travel has not been figured out... at least not publicly. There have been rumors, though. I saw a YouTube video a while back speculating on the possible time travelers throughout history. Some people even think that the people who wrote *The Simpsons* secretly mastered some kind of time traveling mechanism. Did they have some sort of knowledge of the future that allowed them to be remarkably spot on about events that occurred after the show was written?

The average person might just think that this is some crazy coincidence, or due to a mystical power that only *The Simpsons* writers have. Whatever the reason, as far as we know, time only moves in one direction (and no, I'm not talking about the boy band). It's a one-way street, and that way is forward. Some people might argue that we never have enough time. Compared to the rest of history, a single human life is fleeting. It is the blink of an eye – if that – held up next to the age of the universe. Yet, we still focus our time on insignificant people and meaningless situations.

Growing up, I had a really good friend named Harry, and Harry had a father named John. I spent a lot of time hanging out at Harry's because his house was pretty damn cool. Harry's family had a pool, a ping pong table, an air hockey table, and of course, a PlayStation.

What more could you want and need at thirteen years old?

Harry's house was sleepover central. It was the Mecca of slumber parties. We spent many nights watching movies, eating popcorn, and calling girls then immediately hanging up because we were too scared to talk to them. We always had a grand old time whenever we hung out. While I probably went over there about seventy times, I only met his dad once.

It confused me for a while, and I finally got off the balls to ask. "Harry, just curious, does your dad actually live here?" I didn't want to bring up anything crazy that might be going on within his family relationships, but he was my friend and I did want to know.

Harry was quiet after I asked. He gave me a strange look. "What kind of question is that?!" he asked. I guess it was close to the type of response I'd expected. "Of course he lives here!"

"Okay," I said, "How come I've only met him once in over five years?"

Harry went into a long, drawn out story to explain why. He said that his dad did international work for an international company doing all of these international-type things in international places… or at least that was what I got from it. Harry told me that his dad's goal in life was to retire at a young age. Of course, when you're 16 years old, you don't think of 45 as a young age. I can tell you, though, as 35-year-old at the time that I'm writing this book, 45 does seem like a young age. Well, at least we can act like it is.

Basically, Harry told me that his dad's reason for working double time, rarely being home, and constantly traveling overseas was so he could make a ton of extra money and retire to a place on the beach. It seemed like a nice plan, but even though Harry's family was pretty well off, he had never once seen the ocean. I thought this was absolutely crazy. They lived in this nice house and had a nice car that no one ever drove. What was the point in having all of those nice things if you never actually enjoyed them? What was the point in providing so much for your family if you never actually got to spend time with them? To me, it seemed like his dad was so trapped and so badly wanted to retire that he couldn't even stop to enjoy all the money he was making. He couldn't even take a few days to spend time with his son, or at least appreciate the incredible home he lived in.

Harry's father had all these things, sure, but it wasn't enough for him... not yet. He would only truly be happy when he was retired and living on the beach.

Fast forwarding a few years, Harry and went to college. One day, Harry came into my dorm room with one of the biggest grins I'd ever seen.

"What's up?" I asked.

"I'm finally going to be able to spend more time with my dad!" said Harry. "We're going to move to the beach – he's retiring!"

"Oh, that's fantastic!" I said. Still, I was a little skeptical. Harry's dad had only seen his son maybe five days out of the year, would all that really change?

Despite my skepticism, Harry's dad did end up retiring. He and Harry's mom moved to the beach, finally fulfilling John's life-long dream. It was a lovely house, with a view of the ocean and the scent of salty air blowing past. John had finally reached paradise.

Just two days after move-in, Harry's mom made breakfast for her newly-retired husband. As she brought that meal to where he lay in bed, she nudged him to wake him. John didn't respond. Thinking he was playing some kind of joke, Harry's mom nudged him again. John remained still. Sadly, at the age of 51, Harry's father had died in his sleep.

This story still brings tears to my eyes. I tell you this not out of some morbid sense of wanting to shock you, but to demonstrate a little of what I'm talking about when I say to live in the moment. The truth of the matter is that we work our asses off, day in and day out, because we are trying to live for the *future*, and not for *today*. Obviously, I wouldn't tell you to quit your job tomorrow. I'm telling you to have a plan. As you live your life, whether you work in an office, at home, or a zoo, do something new every day. Enjoy what you can in the every day. Don't just expect to be happy when you "arrive" at some specific destination. Think about it like a hike. While it's fine to have a destination, the best hikes aren't through barren wastelands with no scenery. You hike past trees, and rivers, and waterfalls. It's not about one item, or one point on a map. That item is all in your head. So, arrive today. Be happy today, and don't wait.

Sometimes, we find ourselves being paralyzed by our pasts, or obsessed with the future. One of these has already happened, and one of these doesn't even freaking exist yet! Still, the average human spends seventy percent of their precious time trapped in one of those two places. Also, remember that seventy percent of all statistics are made up on the spot.

Now, why is it that we tend to focus so much on the future? Why do we care so much about something that doesn't even exist yet, when we are perfectly capable of enjoying that which we already have? This impossible-to-reach time is so important to the average person because we are always told – by the media, by our parents, and by our teachers – that we must focus on our future. Pick a school and a job that's best for your future. Don't forget to save up for the future!

Just as strong of a focus is the past. Social media is always asking you to "remember when," and those older than us love to talk about the "good old days." It seems that no matter what time period we are in, right *now* will never be enough. It's so true that they even coined a few phrases used in everyday life:

"Time flies when you're having fun!"

"Seems like just yesterday..."

"Time waits for no one."

"That flew by."

Who knows why we love to focus on all the times that aren't *right now*? Maybe it's because our minds love to latch on to the things that are not right in front of us. It could be the same reason why our restless brains love to wander, leading to us to have thoughts about everything... including our own thoughts.

Do you ever find yourself wondering why your teen years seemed to last for twenty years, yet the past three years felt like three months? How is it possible to blink and miss a decade of your life? Believe it or not, there's a scientific reason for this paradoxical phenomenon. Apparently, our minds get caught in a repetitive loop. If we do the same things day in and day out, then time moves very fast. If you are someone who wakes up, goes to work (taking the same route every time), and comes home at about the same time every day, you might know a little bit about what I'm talking about when I refer to this loop.

This loop forces your mind into a pattern. If you do the same thing or think the same thoughts all the time, then time will appear to pass by quickly. And you will never get those hours and minutes back. That time will be wasted. When you're young and experiencing new things, all of that "new" time won't be something you've experienced before. It will seem to go a lot slower. Once you grow up, you'll get into a routine. You'll repeat the same thing every day. You'll get into a routine. You'll repeat the same thing every day. You'll get into a routine. You'll repeat the same thing every day. It will make it harder to enjoy *the every day*, so you'll start searching for time to make you happy.

Sometimes, we act like reaching some mystical point in our life will fix everything. It's as if our unhappiness at our jobs or relationships will be cured by attaining a specific goal. Well, my friends, this is one of the biggest mistakes that any of us can make. Relying on happiness in the future is like relying on a happiness unicorn. That's because – as much as I hate to tell you this – the future does not exist. And honestly, the past doesn't exist either. The past only exists in your own memory, and the future only exists in your imagination because it hasn't happened yet.

So, I have a challenge for you. Stop trying to box everything you do into the "I'm gonna be happy when…" mindset. Instead, be grateful for the happiness you experience right *now*. Go through life assuming that you have already made it. You've done everything you've ever wanted to do, and accomplished all your goals. Sometimes, the universe does step in and finds a way of helping you reach your ultimate end goal.

And sometimes the universe will cause the time to truly fly by.

The COVID-19 pandemic disrupted so much in our lives, including time. For about a year during that time, my wife and I spent much more time inside than we were used to. Throughout the many hours we spent inside together, I often told my wife, "Time just been dragging on."

If you haven't heard what COVID is, then I recommend you climb out from under that rock you've been living under and Google it. If you don't know what Google is, then ask someone older than you. Just know that thanks to COVID, we were stuck inside for long stretches of time, hoping to prevent the spread of a deadly disease.

Though this period lasted a year, it felt more like two or three years. It could have been the stress of a deadly virus weighing down on time itself, but I think part of the reason it seemed to move so slowly was that we were experiencing something new every day. The news gave us something different to focus on. We found new internet trends to try out. Being stuck inside, we moved a little less… and so did time.

While I don't necessarily recommend being on lockdown during a global pandemic, I do think that we can all learn from the situation. If anything, I learned to take each day at a time. Living in the future during COVID was hard when that future was so uncertain, so I had no choice but to live in the moment. You can still plan for the future, of course, but don't dwell on it. Don't build a house on those shifting sands. You can maybe bask there on occasion, but any building you try to establish there will collapse, I promise you. Live with the little things that surround you *now*. Focus on the solid, real things, like your family, friends, and the people you care about. Don't let the angst and worry about the future ruin your present moment… because it hasn't happened yet. After all, they do say that seventy-five percent of the things we worry about never even happen.

And of course, don't be trapped in your past. Don't be trapped somewhere that doesn't exist anymore. Dwelling on things that have already happened is like staying in a prison without walls. There's no reason to remain in a place that isn't there.

So, don't a victim of your past, or be lost in the undecided future. Be present.

You know the age-old phrase: "they call it the present because it's a gift." You wouldn't (or at least you shouldn't) waste a gift. You wouldn't throw at a perfectly good sweater in the trash. You wouldn't let a car sit in the driveway if you received it from your spouse. So, don't waste the time you have! The only thing that is guaranteed is right now. All you have is this moment, the one in which you are reading this book. Cherish the time you spend with the people you care about. And those activities you love the most? Hold onto those when you're doing them. You never know when it is that will be the last time you do it.

# CHAPTER 7:

# YOU CAN'T PUT HAPPINESS IN YOUR SHOPPING CART

For ten years, I have been in my current position in commission sales. I've met a lot of salespeople, or people who were *technically* in sales, but not actually selling. The people I've met come in all shapes, sizes, and personality types. Most of the new commission sales reps went from making little to no money at their jobs to soon making more money than they had ever dreamed they would. They have all kinds of backgrounds, too. Some of them were plumbers, garbagemen, servers, hole diggers, and car salesmen. Many of them, of course, are high school and college dropouts who never really had tax-paying jobs.

In getting to know a lot of these individuals, I noticed they all shared one thing: money problems. It wasn't the normal money problems, like not being able to make mortgage payments or pay a phone bill. It wasn't that they didn't have enough money, but that they did not know what to do with the money they had. Once they got it, they didn't know what the source of their happiness even was.

One of the guys I've met is Adam, who was born in Alabama. He got his start laying asphalt in the dead heat of Florida summers. He was a high school dropout and was making about $31,000 a year for himself, his three kids, and his wife. He was the sole breadwinner, as his wife was disabled and had to take care of the kids. He had, on average of about one week off every two months, as well as most every Sunday off.

He was recommended to me by someone else, so Adam moved to Tennessee to work the same commission sales as me. He was an awesome guy and a great family man. He was a hard worker, too. In his first month in sales, Adam earned $31,500 in commission.

I'll never forget the day Adam came to my office with tears in his eyes. I can still hear Adam in that thick Alabama accent: "Josh, this be $500 more in one month that I've ever made in an entire year." He had to say it at least six times, too, because he didn't believe it for himself. Or maybe he didn't think I could understand him.

I didn't need to listen through that thick accent, or even speak the same language, to understand what that meant to him. I could see it painted on his face. That was what my job provided for Adam and others. I was blessed to work there.

Fast forwarding, Adam had a great next couple of years. On average, he was making around $300,000 annually. He bought his family a house in Tennessee, and they left Florida. They could now afford all kinds of nice things, and could take great vacations as a family. Adam bought himself a nice new Rolex watch and brand new Ferrari. He was living the life so many of us can only dream about.

A couple years into his employment, Adam came to me in tears once again. This time, the tears flowed for a different reason. His home life was not the dream you might think it was for a man with a large house, a Rolex watch, and a Ferrari. Adam's wife was always yelling at him, and his kids were telling him that they never saw him anymore.

"Josh," he said to me, "I'm the unhappiest I've ever been."

At the time, I was shocked to hear it. I could not understand it. How could he be unhappier now than he was when he was struggling to provide for a family of four with an income of $31,000 a year? How could he feel that way after toiling in the hot sun for so long?

The truth was that Adam, like many other people, forgot where true happiness resided. He was making money for the sake of making money. He was focused on the numbers, and on the things he could buy with that income, instead of making himself happy. He had forgotten that the majority of his happiness did not come from his sports car, or his gold watch, but from the less shiny, everyday things. Happiness came from getting to see his son sink the winning basket that took his basketball team to state. Happiness came from sharing a meal around the dinner table, from Sunday afternoon drives, or from sitting on the couch to watch a movie. Sure, working that late night might have gotten him more money, but it could not buy the happiness that came with seeing his last grandparent when they came to town for dinner.

I have always been a person that has demanded success. In fact, I sometimes preach it. Like Adam with his shiny watch and roaring car, I'm definitely a person who likes nice things. I am not someone, however, who relies on those nice things to ultimately make me happy. I will lie in my emotions. I rely on my strong willpower. I will remember the little things that make me happy and use them to get to where I need to be.

Money is not the reason we work our asses off, but it allows us to ensure that our lives are fulfilled. It lets us spend more time with our families or the people we love. It lets us do the things we actually we care about, like getting a twelve-pack of White Claws and attempting to play eighteen holes of drunk golf with our old college buddies, or hunting deer on the weekend. Sure, make that extra dollar on the weekend, but if you bail on your college buddies every time they ask you to play golf with them (even though you *promised* you'd go this time), that might just make you an asshole. You reminding them that you made $31,000 last month is probably not going to make them think you are any less of an asshole.

Adam was not the first example, nor will he be the last example of this kind of money problem. I've met all kinds of people at my job who have had success, only to hear them say that they wished they could quit and go back to their old job. For a while, it would blow my mind whenever I heard it. Why would someone want to make *less* money? Why would you want to go back to a position where you made a fraction of what you make now?

It took me a while to understand, but eventually it clicked. After analyzing these colleagues' experiences, and getting to know who these people were, I finally figured out what the hell was going on. These individuals were not delusional, as I had suspected at first. The simple the truth was that they lost the direction of their happiness. Having the weekend off suddenly gave them more happiness than that $250,000 sports car ever could. The reason for their happiness was no longer focused on the *what*, but on the *why*.

Even though these regretful colleagues were successful, and most of them overall good people, the problem was not that they were able to buy nice things and provide for their family. That part is fantastic and life changing. The issue was that most of them lost focus of the *why* behind the job, not the *what*. They saw the sparkling objects that get advertised in magazines, or the things you can put in a shopping cart. They forgot about the things that had *actual* value – the things you can't buy with a credit card. They put all their stock into feeling good. They focused their accomplishments on getting their hands on the fun shiny things:

- New boats
- Diamond Rolexes
- Oversized houses
- Impractical fancy sports cars

Alright, I'll admit, that last one is on me.

To play the devil's advocate, I'll admit that it is true that you do not always have to sacrifice time for money. But that is not the point. The point is that we can no longer try to find the happiness in *what* we have rather than *why* we have it.

"So, Josh, you're telling me that if I have a nice watch I should feel bad about myself?"

Absolutely not. You should feel fantastic and accomplished. I'm sure you worked very hard for that exquisite timepiece. Just remember that, as corny as it sounds, happiness is a state of mind. Happiness is not the diamonds on your Rolex, or the stitching on your designer handbag, or the caviar you eat for dinner every night.

I'll say it again: I love a nice, fancy watch as much as a rapper blingin' out in an Escalade on 28-inch rims. There is nothing wrong with having overpriced or extra nice things. So, what the hell does all this mean? It means that life will continue to mess with you. It won't stop throwing unexpected messes in your face. Even on your good days, something or someone will still try to swoop in and ruin it.

We all have bad days. They're about as unavoidable as Mondays. Might as well accept those days. For me, when I get flipped off by somebody who cut me off, or maybe get a flat tire, it's not the things I have that make me feel better. I can't just look down at my $35,000 watch and say, "Man, I sure feel like a piece of shit today. But at least I have a Rolex!" These items can and will make you happy for a while, but it won't last forever. In the end, these items are like sugar. They sure taste good, and make you feel great in the moment, but if you rely on them to give you life, you'll shut down. You need actual nutrients to keep you going.

So remember, happiness is a state of mind, not an item with a price tag.

# CHAPTER 8:

# THE PAST IS IN THE PAST

**W**e spend a lot of our time thinking about things that we can no longer control. Maybe we think about that spelling bee we could have won if we had just remembered the second "R" in "embarrass." Maybe we imagine what life would have been like if we had gone to that big state school instead of that college in our hometown. Dwelling on this sort of thing is just plain silly, though. That doesn't mean it's not hard to avoid thinking this way, because we are humans. As I'm sure you know, humans are goofy creatures. We have strong emotions, which makes it hard to control them. It's a long process to be able to harness this desire to dwell on the past, but a good way to start is by simply saying, "It is what it is."

This helps us avoid the mistake of wanting to go back and change it. Why is it so important to avoid this desire? Because, well, WE CAN'T! So, just stop it. Move forward instead of getting stuck or going backward. Don't be haunted by the way things were, or how it use to be, or the "good ol' days." Because all you can do is learn, and then take what you've learned and improve. Never let a good today be ruined by a bad yesterday.

You may have heard the phrase "Hindsight is 20/20" and wondered, "What the hell does that mean?" It's basically saying that it's easy to know the right thing to do after something has happened. Well, no freaking shit! Sorry, I get I little worked up, but it seems to me that people just throw this saying around without even knowing what it means. We do that with a lot of sayings, just because we heard them once.

As I've mentioned before, human beings haven't (that we know of) invented a time machine. You can change the past about as much as you can change the rotation of the earth. All you can do is hope that you make the best decision with the information you have at the time. Then, all you can do is live with the results. If the results of whatever decision you make are not what you want, then guess what? Learn from that mistake in the future. That is the only way to ever get better.

Still, you might sometimes feel the urge to use a time machine. There have been plenty of people who made movies about the ability to travel through time. Some viewers may have even believed that it was possible. But if it is, I haven't been given access to it.

When I was a teenager, I saw *The Time Machine* movie made in 2003. I was so fascinated by this. I couldn't stop wondering about what it would be like for someone to be able to travel back in time. I was so fascinated that I spent the next year researching. I watched countless YouTube videos about it. I found as many movies as I could about time travel. Of course, I have now memorized nearly every line from the *Back to the Future* movies.

As intrigued as I was by the idea of changing the past, I began to wonder if that was really something I would want to do. Sure, you might say to me, "Josh, I would go back in time and bet on a baseball game or other sports event. I would be mega wealthy!"

Think about what you would really do, though. If you could go back, would you really make some money off a game, or spend time with someone you care about? Would you go back to work harder, or go back to tell someone what you think about them? You could spend days trying to figure what you would do if you could go back, but dwelling on it too much would just make you sadder.

My father had me in his late 40s and he passed away at the age of 77. I was only 28 when I had to say goodbye. Though I felt like I got to spend a lot of time with him doing some of the things we both love, I couldn't help but wonder... did I really spend enough time with him? Should I have gone to breakfast with him a few more times? Should I have gone with him when he asked me to hang out instead of doing the dumb things that dumb twenty-year-olds want to do? Maybe I got mad too much. Maybe I yelled at him when I shouldn't have. There were a multitude of things I probably shouldn't have done, but what was important was that I was close to my dad. Some people don't even have that. I had the privilege of knowing that he loved me more than he loved himself. Anything that I have now and everything that I do today are thanks to him. He is one, or many, of those pieces that make up who I am today. Having him in my life truly made me a better person. That is all that matters. What I should and shouldn't have done isn't what's important. Because no matter what you do, you could have always done more.

I want to encourage you to think about what you are grateful for – not what you could have or should have done. Wherever you are in your life, and whenever you think about the past, remember that it is what it is. You are the way you are for a reason. If you're not the person you want to be, use the past as a tool. Learn from what you've seen and done and shape yourself a better future.

Your days are short. With every rotation of the Earth, you are a little bit older. So, it's important to understand how pointless it is to fret about the past. Don't sit and worry and wish... take action!

# CHAPTER 9:

# STOP WANTING WHAT YOU DON'T HAVE

**W**e all want things. We've wanted things since we were little. When we are born, we want to be swaddled. When we are kids, we wanted sugar. When we were in high school, we want the coolest new clothes, and as adults, we want the nicest house. It's natural. Many of us, though, want what we don't have. We even want things to happen that won't happen. We can never truly be happy, though, in that mental state. You've probably heard the phrase, "You want what you can't have." And that's true for all ages of our lives, from year one to one hundred and one.

Speaking of year one, that happens to be the age of my son at the time of this writing. To be exact, he is eighteen months old. That is about a year and a half, for people like me who have trouble with math. Anyway, having a child is not a joke. It might have hilarious, absurd moments, but it's nothing to scoff at. And no matter how many parents you talk to, or how many kids you babysit, you will never really know what It's like until you have a kid of your own. Once you find yourself covered in every bodily fluid imaginable and functioning on less sleep in a week than you usually got in a day, all while raising a brand new human being, you will realize that the word "doozy" does not even cover it.

One thing I've learned as a father is that if my son has a nice toy in front of him, there is always something shinier and more fun out there. If he sees me with something, be it a TV remote, a knife for cutting chicken, or even a beer, my kid will want it. The second I move this coveted item away after he reaches toward it, he will start to cry. It's pretty common for kids his age, but it doesn't go away as we become adults. It just intensifies, even if we get a little better at hiding it.

Wanting what you don't have is different from wanting what you *can't* have. Speaking for myself, I'm a fighter and a go-getter. If someone tells me I can't do something, I will go out of my way to try to prove them wrong. A lot of people with "type A" personalities are like this. They want things they don't have, which is different from things they will never reach. Saying that you *can't* have some things, like a mansion, a fancy car, or a hotter girlfriend or boyfriend wouldn't be true. Anything is possible if you work hard for it. Put your mind and effort into it, and you will find a way to get it. What causes so many of us to live unsatisfying lives, though, is that we aren't satisfied with the things we *do* have... even when we end up getting something that we've always wanted.

When I first started my current job, I was 26 years old. All throughout my teen years and my early twenties, my dream car was a Land Rover Range Rover. I often said to myself, "Man, when I have this, I'll be the shit. Well, when I turned twenty-seven on Christmas, I bought this car for myself after one year of success at my new job.

For the first six or so months, I was absolutely thrilled every time I got into the car. However, I found myself filled with envy on a nice June day as I drove with the windows down. I stopped at a traffic light when something pulled up beside me. It was a Range Rover. It was similar to the one I was sitting in at the time, but it was a newer model.

Oh man.

It was incredible. I couldn't help but think about how cool it would be if I had that car instead. In my head, the car next to me was completely different from mine. It was shinier. It was sleeker. I was sure it could go faster. But truthfully, if I really examined it, that car did not look that much different from mine. In fact, the body style was the same. It had four wheels and a windshield, but the lights in the front and back were different. Still, for the next day, and maybe even week, I could not keep myself from thinking about how cool it would be to save up and get that other car. I felt like I wouldn't be satisfied until I got it.

So, fast forward another year, and *bam*! I rolled up to my house with that newer Range Rover model that had pulled up next to me the year before. It was an awesome car. I was awesome for having that awesome car. I even remember saying that I was probably going to have this until the time I had kids within the next two or three years.

Then, another year went by and guess what? I no longer wanted an SUV. I wanted a sports car.

Ain't that a bitch? How shocking. Me... not satisfied.

Like a moth having been drawn to light, I found myself on Auto Trader searching for cars. I decided that I wanted to get an Audi R8. If you don't know, the R8 is a pretty sweet car, and about six months later that sweet car was in my driveway. I drove that around for about a year before I decided I just did not want a sports car as my everyday vehicle. Looking back, I probably should have just kept the Range Rover, but that's beside the point.

I was in constant search of what I thought would make me happy. I just kept purchasing cars because that was what I felt good about at the time... or at least what I *thought* I felt good about. I was constantly thinking that I had something to prove. And I *was* proving something, but it wasn't that I was cool, or special, or high tech, but that I had no idea what the hell I was doing. I was spending like a rockstar. Yes, I did have some money, but it was nowhere near what a rockstar has.

I do not regret having those nice cars, but what I say to you is this: be careful how you think. Be careful with what you view as the *next thing*. Are you really doing something because you feel like it's going to move you further in your life and toward your financial goals? Do you pursue things that will help your relationships with your friends and family, or are you doing it just because you're bored? I know, I know, I can hear you already: "Josh, how bored does one have to be to spend $450,000 on 3 cars in 3 years?" I'm using "bored" as a loose term. I think of it kind of like a *board*game.

Now that we're on that topic, is it really called a boardgame because it is typically on some kind of cardboard, or because you have to be bored to play it? I don't really know, but I can Google it later. It's probably a mixture of both.

What I'm trying to say is that we often play boardgames when we want to occupy our minds. We'll pull one out when there's a lull in the conversation after a dinner party. We'll dust it off if there's nothing else to do. It satiates our constantly running minds, seeing as our minds are constantly looking for the next thing. Now, nothing wrong with board games of course, but if you find yourself relying on this, or anything else, as an escape from your every day, try to remember this: you are where you are supposed to be. You are in the current moment – not in the future, and not in the past. You are in the present.

The bottom line is that I don't care how many things you have, there's always going to be someone with a bigger boat, nicer muscles, fancier cars, a nicer house, or a cat with better teeth. Whatever the hell it is, there's always going to be something else. Your mind is a crazy place, and will have you wondering why you can't have better things. I'm not saying you should not want nicer things. I'm not telling you not to work extra hard. I'm all about that. But if you start going after more and more things just *because*, like I did, you won't find true happiness.

Your brain is kind a suitcase you might take on a trip. There is only so much room in your head, so don't fill it with too many things that would make your travels more difficult. Don't trash your thoughts with harmful ideas, like the assumption that you're not where you need to be. Stop thinking about the fact that you don't have what you want. Are there things that other people have that are better than yours? Well, too bad. Because that will always be the case. Once you start to appreciate all the things you do have, you will begin to see the things you never saw before. You will begin to learn what truly matters.

# CHAPTER 10:

# PROCRASTINATION

Ah, procrastination.

Whether you're a school student waiting until the day it's due to start an assignment, or a worker beginning a project twenty minutes before your boss wants it on her desk, or a boyfriend holding off on proposing after many years together, guess what? You're a procrastinator!

If you think about it, it's kind of silly to procrastinate considering the simple fact that you'll see on the cover of this book: you're gonna die soon. You'll "do it later?" Who even knows what later is! You could be hit by bus, or have a heart attack, or be struck by a meteorite tomorrow. You're not going to be around forever. I'm not trying to make you sad – in fact, I tell you that to do the opposite. Once you realize that "later" might not even exist, your life will change for the better. It will get you thinking and focusing on different things. Plus, there is an art to procrastination. It's something that almost every human being in existence does at some time. It could be in their day-to-day life, or once in a while. We sometimes don't even realize when we do it.

Growing up, I had a friend whose mom would say, "My diet starts next week." Except, she would say it *every* week, and always while eating three packs of Nutty Buddies. Now, let's be real, Nutty Buddies are freaking delicious. But the last time I saw my friend's mom, which was a couple years ago, she unfortunately was not getting any smaller. Am I being rude by saying this? Absolutely not. She was being rude to herself. For years, she tried to trick herself into thinking that she was actually going to start a diet, but never took the necessary actions to get her closer. In fact, she would actually talk herself out of dieting, because every time she would eat something extra unhealthy, she would justify it by saying that the diet would start in just a few days.

You may not think of yourself as a salesperson, but in a way, all of us are. We all sell ourselves every day. You sell yourself reasons why you should or should not go to the gym. You sell reasons to eat or not to eat breakfast. You sell yourself reasons why you should or should not stay at work.

You may have not realized it until now, but we are all sales-people. You can be a salesperson even when you are alone and in bed. If you have the sudden realization that you forgot to brush your teeth, you may end up selling the importance of putting your feet onto the cold ground and heading to the bathroom at the cost of leaving your warm and comfy spot under the blankets. It's not the toothbrush or Colgate convincing you to get up and brush your teeth. It's you.

This is all to say that procrastination is the art of selling yourself. Procrastination involves telling yourself why the current thing you're doing is better than the future thing you *should* be doing... or not doing. There is hope, though. I find that one of the best ways to get over procrastination is to just start. Whether you start without finishing, start without any real destination, or start even without knowing what you're doing... you're still starting. The way to start to losing weight is by eating one less slice of pizza, or one less donut. You don't have to completely stop eating pizza or completely stop eating donuts. But one less is one step closer to watching your weight.

Procrastination uses fear and stalling to hold you back. Most people end up doing the things that they procrastinate. They spend a lot of time worrying and stressing and sweating and using up that precious commodity that is their life. Seeing that the title of this book is *You're Gonna Die Soon*, I'll take this time to remind you that *you're gonna die soon*. Stop pushing off things that you know you need to be doing. It's time. Just do it! You don't even have to be wearing Nikes to do most of these things. Take action today! Because you can't finish until you start.

# CHAPTER 11:

# YOU'RE NOT THE ONLY ONE WITH PROBLEMS

In May of 2021, Bill and Melinda Gates announced that they were getting divorced. At the time, Bill Gates was worth 130 billion dollars – primarily from the founding of the company Microsoft. I'm sure many of you have heard of it. And, in case you were not aware, $130 billion is a lot of money. It's an amount that they say is hard to spend in a lifetime, or even three lifetimes. And, because of interest, his net worth goes up every day. It happens without the need for Bill to even get off the couch.

According to some of the articles I read about their divorce, their problems allegedly stemmed from some of the same issues that most marriages fall victim to: kids, chores, and wanting to do different things. There were other theories, about the reason for their divorce, but the fact of the matter is this: it doesn't matter your age, race, country of origin, or how wealthy you are, your problems are not special or unique. You'll have problems in all aspects of your life.

What's important is the things you are focusing on – and why. Are you looking for a solution, or are you just looking for a problem for the sake of having a problem? I learned long ago that I should not focus on the problems and challenges that I could not fix. When I did focus on those things I couldn't fix, I often found myself worried about the silliest things.

Maybe you spend a week telling yourself that you need to go for a walk, then on the day you decide to head out of the house, it's raining outside. This might ruin your whole day. But, is it really worth worrying about, considering the fact that there is nothing you can do to fix it? I wish I could tell you that I had Mother Earth on speed dial. I wish I could tell you I could call her up and ask a favor and make the rain wait. But I cannot, nor can you. I must have lost her number years ago.

Now, let's say you're worried about something you can actually fix or change. Let's say you have a job interview next week. You might be upset because you're not sure that it's going to go well. The idea of sitting in front of a stranger and answering questions about your resume might fill you with worry.

The actions that you can take when you have a job interview are making sure your resume is up to par, ensuring you know everything about the company, and practicing your speaking skills in the mirror. There are all kinds of things you can do to prepare. You could research how to do well in an interview. You could learn all there is to know about *yourself*. Now, let's say you've done all of those things, and yet, you're still worried. Well, that's on you, my friend. Don't spend an entire week of your life not being able to sleep or eat because you are constantly thinking about how this interview is going to go. At the end of the day, if you've done everything that you possibly can to make yourself the best imaginable contender, then let fate have it. It will be what it will be, but do not let it take control of your days. Don't give it so much power.

One of the other things I learned long ago was to not worry about anything that is out of my control. Imagine a person is having financial problems, which means they don't have enough money to pay for their electricity. They might be worried it will be turned off, and their kids won't be able to eat. For the most part, this is a problem with a possible solution. That person could borrow money from a friend. They could call the electric company and explain the situation. They could maybe even take a night shift to get a little more income. But, if you're worried that there's going to be a huge storm that will take out your electricity at some point this year, then that's something out of your control.

The point is that most things we worry about are things that are in our control. We often worry about things that we believe are problems we can solve. I know this might surprise you, but I cannot control the weather. I cannot stop it from raining when I go outside, no matter how hard I try, but I can bring an umbrella.

When it comes down to our personal problems, or things that we worry about, we often find ourselves heading into to the "woe is me" scenario. Don't go there, though. Stop thinking that you are special. You are not the only one with problems. I promise you, everyone else in the world isn't out there having the most glorious, carefree life. Everyone else has problems too, they just might not let you see it. Even if you don't see the issues they're facing, remember this: we are all in this life together – through the good *and* the bad. No one gets out alive.

Chances are, if you're working toward a goal, you're not the only person doing so. Look at the person on your left, then look at the person on your right. Both of them have problems. Oh, yeah, look at the person in front of you, too. The one you might envy because you want what he has. Yup, he has problems too. And you know what, his problems might even be worse than yours. You never know what someone else is going through.

You will never meet anyone who has never had any worries or problems. That makes it even more important to be kind to other people, even strangers. It can't hurt to smile at someone you don't know every once in a while. As you're walking down the street, try waving at someone you don't know. See someone struggling? Ask if you can help them accomplish their task. They might be having a really rough week, and a simple action could just change their life forever.

# CHAPTER 12:

# YOUR EXPERIENCE IS YOUR EXPERIENCE

Every day of your life is an experience. You are experiencing something every single second. It may not always be super eventful, but even sitting or sleeping is still an experience. How you choose to respond or react to that experience is up to you. Now, when a baby is crying at the top of their lungs and you are trying to concentrate on writing a book, then yes, it makes that experience a bit more difficult. However, it is still up to you. If you get irritated, you may choose to throw your typewriter to the floor and go punch a wall, as some people have. Obviously, though, that's not the most productive response, and I'm sure your typewriter repairman, handyman, and doctor would all recommend against that course of action.

I met a man named Bob at my first job out of college. Bob was an interesting fella, to say the least. At the time, I was 23, and Bob was a bit older, so we both had different views of the world.

There was one day at work that I'd had it at that job. I was literally on the way to the boss's office to quit. On my way there, I saw Bob sitting in his cluttered cubicle with a stack of reports almost as tall as him. At this point, the AC had broken again, so it was extremely hot. I swerved from my mission and approached Bob, who grinned from ear to ear even though he was drowning in sweat. "How's it hangin', Josh?" he asked.

"Not good, Bob," I said. "Not good at all."

"Why not?" said Bob, almost looking shocked.

"I'm on my way to quit the shitty job! I don't know how you stand it!"

He turned to a four-foot by four-foot poster of a palm tree beach on a beach and said, "Well, I'm in paradise."

I wanted to slap him, but he continued.

"I've always wanted to work on the beach, so this is as good as it gets. I'm happy because I control my thoughts."

At 23, this was pretty shocking to hear. Those words hit me like a wrecking ball (cue Miley Cyrus tune). It really made me think, *Damn. Is it really all in our heads?*

It seems strange, though. You may even be thinking, *Josh that's some horseshit. Sitting in a cubicle next to a poster is difference from being on a beautiful beach with a cold drink in your hand as a breeze blows through your hair.* And sure, I agree. However, your current experience is in your control. Don't waste the days you have trying to hope for the days you don't have yet.

Sure, being on a beach might seem better than being in the office. But just because someone is sitting on the beach doesn't mean they are happy. How can a person be wealthy and be sitting on a beautiful, warm beach, but still be mad at the world? Well, it's possible because just like *you* create your own paradise, you can create your own Hell. It goes where you go. If you choose to be miserable, that will follow you. If I were riding on a bus I might think, *Man, this bus is gross*, while the person right next to me thinks, *Thank God I can afford the bus, or I'd have to walk.* It's all about perspective.

# CHAPTER 13:

# UNNATURAL DISASTERS (MAN-MADE)

**W**e create almost everything that we feel. Other than being hot or cold, we create pretty much everything else. Believe it or not, if you're tired or worn out, this is often all in your head as well.

A placebo is a pill that typically has little, if any, medicinal value. Placebos are simply "fake" pills that professionals may give to patients or subjects, often as part of the control aspect of a study. While placebos don't have the medication found in real pills, patients have still reported that placebos have helped them feel or perform better. But how? How can a *nothing* pill help us? John Kelley, a psychology professor at Endicott College, heads a program on placebo studies. He doesn't view placebos as useless, even if they may not technically contain any form of medicine. That's because for John Kelly, placebos can be a form of psychotherapy.

Now, you might be thinking that a placebo wouldn't really work if you *know* it's fake. But according to Kelley, placebos can work even if the patient knows it's a placebo.

You too can unlock the power of that magical pill… and you don't even need to get some fake medication. Kelley's placebo studies show that placebos themselves aren't necessarily what's powerful – but it's the human mind that has the power.

The mind can be one of the greatest tools in the world, and it can also be one of the worst. In fact, 75 percent of the worst things that have ever happened in my life are things that never actually happened. One of those things involved getting into college. I was so worried about passing the entrance exam that I was sure I'd failed. It ruined almost a month of my life.

One of these moments happened in high school. I was so worried about asking a girl to prom that I almost didn't even go. I was that worried she'd say no.

Another happened after I'd graduated from high school when I worked in sales. My boss wanted to talk to me, but he wanted to wait until he got back from vacation. I was sure I was getting fired, but instead, he gave me a promotion.

Sometimes, the worst part about life is the unknown. The scariest thing we can face is that which we don't understand or know in the moment we want to know it.

Sometimes, things become disasters in our life before they even become reality. You are a byproduct of your past and how you might have been raised, but you are also a direct effect of the thoughts you put in your head. Your thoughts become your reality. So, do not waste your days being upset. You are, of course, allowed to be frustrated, mad, sad, etc. However, remember that life is too short to let it consume you.

# CHAPTER 14:

# WHAT'S LOVE GOT TO DO WITH IT?

It's one of the most common themes you'll ever find.

*Love.*

You've read about it in The Bible, and nearly every movie (even the "manly" ones with action) has it. Everyone, I hope, has felt it to some degree… but sometime, it seems, we lose track of what that really means.

I met my wife Hayley in 2013. We got engaged in 2014 after about eight months of dating, and then got married in May 2015. I very much love my wife. She is so incredibly special to me. And I'm happy to report that I'm pretty confident she feels the same way about me. Throughout my years being married, though, I've noticed a problem in the way that many people view love. There's an assumption that you must actively love the other person 100 percent, all the time, without messing up. But just because you're in love with another person doesn't mean you have to like them every second of every day. In fact, I'm sure there are times that my wife wants to punch me in the face. You may laugh, but this is normal. It doesn't mean you will always be miserable, of course, but to make any type of relationship work, there has to be an understanding.

I'm not going to pretend to be a marriage counselor – I'm not even close to being one! However, over the years, I have learned a lot from friends and other people around me. I know people who have been concerned about their relationships because they were not head over heels in love *all* the time. Maybe you have felt the same way. Maybe you watched a really good romance movie on the Hallmark channel and thought to yourself, "Son of a bitch, I must have married the wrong person. I don't feel that way about my husband (or wife)!"

Maybe you've seen the kind of relationship filled with passion and nonstop sex. The two partners might call each other eight times a day just to hear the other's voice, and to let them know that they cannot live without them. Seems fun, but I've got news for you if you did not already know: love has nothing to do with that. Love is waking up at 3 AM to let the dog out when it's 6° outside, even though you know you won't be able to fall back to sleep. Love is doing that just because you know your partner hates to do it. Love is canceling poker night because eight months before you promised your wife you'd go see *Cats* on Broadway. Love is the messy, frustrating, and unexciting times. It's about being forgiving and understanding. True love is seeing a person who for who they are.

# CHAPTER 15:

## focus

**W**hen the average person thinks of focusing, they think of it as a positive thing. Unfortunately, it is the negative aspect of focus that cripples many people's minds.

Sometimes, it's easier to focus on negative things than it is to focus on positive things. From the moment you wake up, you're hit with bad news on TV, which they love to pump us with. That already starts our mind in a negative focus. Then, you hop in your car thinking:

*I'm going to be late.*

*I bet I'll hit traffic.*

*By the time I leave work it'll be dark out.*

*My boss is probably going to be a jerk again.*

By doing this, you are giving power to negative thoughts.

Try starting every day saying that despite what the day throws at you, regardless of what people say, and that even if the world tries to bring you down, you will hold up your head with a smile. Because you are built to overcome anything.

When it comes to success and fortune, and your desire for a big house and a fancy car, focus on *that*. Make every move you do towards your goal. A few years ago, I decided I would make what some might call a vision or dream board. I took some pictures of things I wanted, places I wanted to go, and the person I wanted to be that year, and I placed them on the board. One of these was an image of a beach that I found on Google, which represented the view from the house that I one day wanted to own. It hung in my closet for three hundred days, making itself known to me every morning when I woke up, and every night when I went to sleep. I saw it *at least* twice a day.

About a year later, I had forgotten about my vision board after the things in my closet obscured it from view. I had also just purchased a house on the beach. As I walked down into the sand, I snapped a photo. That photo sat in my phone for a few weeks, then one day, while scrolling through my pictures, it caught my eye. Something seemed oddly familiar about that photo.

"Holy shit!" I said, turning to my wife.

She gave me that look – that "What is it now?" look. Then, she said, "What's the problem?"

"No problem!" I said. "I just remember where that picture is from!" I ran upstairs and pulled the dream board out of the closet. I put the beach photo I had snapped a few weeks before right next to the beach photo on my dream board.

They were almost exactly the same.

I had goosebumps. From the time of day, to even where the blades of grass fell on the tunes, to the crystal sands, and the greenish-blue sea, the photos were almost identical. It was like magic.

Whether it was fate, or just a crazy coincidence, it demonstrates the importance of staying laser focused. you must put into play and be laser focused on things that you. Every day will throw things in the mix and start focusing on the bad things. But if you focus on the good in everyone and everything you'll find your way in this crazy world.

Some of you will say that the idea of a dream board has more corn than Thanksgiving dinner. Maybe it does. But I'm telling you, it works. It may not work every time, and maybe not for everyone, but some of you who try it will thank me. Just keep in mind, you can't just assemble your board and wait for things to fall in your lap. You'll still have to take the day-to-day actions to build yourself up for success.

# CHAPTER 16:

## IF IT'S TO BE, IT'S UP TO ME: SELF-MOTIVATION

I was home from college one summer and I spent the first couple weeks not really doing anything. I mostly just lazed around, and maybe had a beer with my friends or sat by the pool catching rays.

I remember one of those days like it like was yesterday. The rain was pounding against the window as I sat on the couch watching. I'm not really sure how long I was sitting there. I may have been sitting there for an hour just watching the rain.

Unbeknownst to me, my dad had been in the other room, glancing at me every once in a while. He'd seen me just sitting, watching the drops of water trickling down the window. I will never forget his deep voice all of a sudden saying, "They're not coming."

"Huh? What?" I said, a little startled.

He stood and approached the couch, then said it slower. "Son, I said, "They are *not* coming.""

I was a bit confused as to who "they" were, and why they would be coming here. So, I turned to him and said, "I'm not waiting on anyone."

"Are you sure?" said my father. "Seems like you might be. Because you're certainly not going out there and doing anything for yourself."

I was thrown off by this. "What do you mean?"

"At the start of the summer, you said you were going to spend your time writing songs, or maybe even find a part-time job singing at a restaurant. I haven't seen you write anything in weeks, or even leave the house during the day." We stared at each other, then he asked, "So, have you?"

All I could say was, "Uhhh…"

"Right!" he said. "Nobody is going to do it for you. *They* are not coming to save you. Nothing is going to end up in your lap." He looked to the rain-speckled window. "The biggest motivator lives inside *you*."

All I could say to those words of wisdom was, "Yeah, right, whatever."

But those words stuck with me. I thought about what he'd said. I thought about it over the next week, and I still think about it every day.

Now, I know that when I want something done, I have to do it. *I* have to push and motivate *myself*. And It's the same for everyone else. Sometimes, if we stop long enough, we might forget it. We spend too much time just waiting. Sometimes, we spend hours just staring out the window, not even sure what we're waiting for.

One thing I always remember my dad saying is this: "If you want something done right, son, you gotta do it yourself." You've probably heard that at some point in your life. And he's correct... mostly. About 99.7 percent correct. Most people want nice things, or to feel accomplished, or make money, or have fewer worries, etc. And sometimes, we end up putting most of our faith in someone else. We think that another person will help us accomplish the things we want.

Now, I am a firm believer in the concept of mentors. We all need wisdom and advice – or someone who has gone through it already. We can't expect that mentor to do it *for* us, though. *No one* will ever want what's best for you more than you. This means it's *your* responsibility to take action. Sorry, but you can't sit around waiting for Publishers Clearing House to knock on your door and hand you a giant check. If you're too young to know what the heck Publishers Clearing House is, then maybe I should say, "Winning the lottery." We all know what that is.

My point is that you can't sit around and wait for things to happen. You have to fight for what you want.

# CHAPTER 17:

# SHIT HAPPENS

I'm not really sure how the phrase started, but a long time ago – possibly in the Middle Ages, or Ancient Egypt, or maybe even during caveman times – people have been saying, "Shit happens." They've said it ever since my mom and dad were kids, at least. They would say it whenever something happened that they didn't want to deal with, and it was usually something they didn't have emotional ties to. Maybe someone was carrying in groceries and knocked over the lamp, sending it crashing to the ground.

"Well, shit happens!"

When that old lady hits your bumper and dings it, you'll hear it too:

"Well, shit happens!"

What is the true meaning of this ancient proverb? What is the "shit" that they refer to... and what is it that actually "happens"?

A few years ago, I took this phrase and added a little something of my own. Now, when *shit happens,* I say, "Well, shit happens. You analyze it, and then you either fix it or you forget it." Because the crazy part is that the *shit* you don't like is going to *happen* every day of your life. Even if you, like a lot of us, try to start your day on a good note by saying, "This is gonna be a great day," shit is still going to happen. You might wake up to the sound of birds chirping outside and tell yourself that everything about the day is going to be beautiful, then end up stubbing your toe the bed as you go to brush your teeth. It could all be downhill from there.

Maybe you misplace your keys on the way to work, so you race out of the driveway because you're running late. As you do, you hit your own mailbox with your brand new car, but can't stop to fix it because if you're any later your boss will fire you. It sucks. But it all could have been solved by one simple phrase: *shit happens*.

You should have worked on your mindset as soon as you bumped your toe. When *shit* like that *happens*, that is not the time to tell yourself it's going to be a terrible day. Instead, just take it in stride and understand that every day you wake up there's going to be some shitty point (or points) throughout the day.

I've learned my lesson, because I'm always ready for it. In fact, sometimes I'll just laugh and say, "Yup, this is probably going to be a shitty day at some point." But sometimes I'll be pleasantly surprised. It ends up not nearly as shitty as I'd thought it was going to be. And when it ends up that way, it makes me happy. It's not necessarily about trying to avoid all the bad shit, but about embracing that the shittiness is a part of life. As you make your way through life, it's probably going to happen to you every day. But you are in control. Do not let the "shit" take control of you.

By embracing the idea that things will be shitty, you will gain the ability to work through it. It will help you roll though some very tough times, and sometimes even let you laugh in the face of the bullshit. Yes, there will be times that are a lot harder to overcome than others. We have all been guilty of saying we were not going to let something bother us, only for it to do just that. So, remember that when this happens, you are only human. We *all* go through it. I don't know how many times I've tried to mentally block something out and not let it affect me, only for my mind to become overpowered.

Everything will work out as long as your foundation is solid. Make sure it is built on the idea that everywhere you go, there's going to be a giant shit show at some point. There's going to be a lot of bullshit to deal with. Don't try to avoid it, because that's not how you win. The way to defeat it is by learning how to manage it.

# CHAPTER 18:

# WHO ARE YOUR REAL FRIENDS?

A in't that a great question? Be careful who you call your "friends." Social media has got us thinking we have thousands of "friends," even if we haven't met some of them.

Speaking of social media, I once had around 5,500 friends on Facebook. Around that time, I was posting pictures of the places I went on vacation, shared some of the accolades I'd received at work, and talked about how grateful I was. Eventually, I noticed that I had around 4,800 friends – which I do not think was a coincidence. It seems unlikely that 700 people would suddenly delete their Facebook accounts.

Many people who claim to be your friends are only your friends when things are convenient. If you're always the person reaching out to someone asking to hang out, go a week without saying anything. See what happens. Sometimes, you'll be shocked. Often, the people you thought were your friends only just happen to go out with you because it's convenient or because they don't want to feel bad by saying no.

It may sound obvious, but if you are always the one reaching out, or if your friend is always looking for an excuse to be busy, then that other person is probably not your friend. The great news is that you do not need to un-friend this person on social media. All you have to do is move on and know that this person is an acquaintance.

Find comfort in knowing that this life goes in many directions. There are so many stages. Just because you hung out with another person at one point in your life, it doesn't mean it has to stay that way. If you or someone else has moved on, or gotten distant, it's not necessarily something to be sad about. It doesn't necessarily mean you did something wrong. It is natural for people to move on. So, don't take it personally.

I tell you that because I *did* take it personally at one point in my life. As a young adult, if I thought I was friends with someone, only to go a year and not hear from them, I would think it was a personal slight against me. I learned over time, though, that stuff like that just happens. The world gets busy. Life gets busy.

The people who truly care about you will reach out to you from time to time. It might just be to check in by text, email, or phone, but it's still a way to show they care.

Trust is a huge a factor in a lot of friends' relationships. For me, breaking that has a profoundly negative effect on a relationship. However, understand that people do like to talk. People like to have a good story. Sometimes, that story might be about you. So, if you do not want your story or your secret to be known, I would share it with no one, or almost no one. I often say that everyone has that one friend they trust. But if *everyone* has that one friend they trust, and you tell two people, all of a sudden four people know. Soon, six people will know, and before you know it, your super secretive secret will be known by half your office.

# CHAPTER 19:

## GUILTY BY ASSOCIATION

When I was kid, my parents used to always tell me to be careful who I associated with. Often, this came in the form of the phrase, "Guilty by association."

I didn't know what this meant at first. For a while, I thought it didn't have much to do with me. That phrase sounded like some fancy law thing that I would never have to worry about.

That changed in middle school, though. At the time, I was spending a lot of time hanging out with a friend, who I'll call, "Ricky," and a friend of Ricky's, who I'll call "John." Ricky, John, and I were riding bikes around the neighborhood. As we rode by someone's driveway, John spotted something shiny in someone else's driveway. It was a bike, and it was much nicer than his.

John wanted that shiny, new bike.

So, John rode into that driveway and set his down. Then, he picked up the shiny new bike and rode off. A bike for a bike!

Nothing wrong with that… except for the fact that it's stealing. John could have been a lawyer. He justified it by saying he was merely borrowing the bicycle. He had a plan to return it. Even with my young, pre-developed brain, I felt like something was a little fishy about this "arrangement."

Still, I kept riding alongside John and Ricky. I was quiet, though. I had determined that something was not right about the situation, but before I could decide what to do, I heard someone yell, "Hey, you!"

A minivan driving next to us sped up, then cut us off. I heard a voice call through the open window. "That's my bike!"

Well, this spooked John and Ricky. They threw down their bicycles and ran. They tore across the lawn of a nearby house and disappeared. Meanwhile, I was there on my bike (that I owned) while staring in bewilderment. The kid, whose bike had been stolen, was sitting in the car bawling his eyes out, all while pointing at *me*.

Even though I hadn't even touched the bike, or condoned it, or even fled when confronted, this kid still blamed me. Trying to plead my case only made things worse. The boy and his mother really did not believe me, but they gave me a pass anyway. They took the bike back, put it in the back of the minivan, and pulled away.

Unfortunately, even though I thought I was a pretty good kid, the boy whose bike had been stolen went to my school. John, the real culprit, did not go to that school. Every time that kid would see me in the hall, I felt like he wanted me to implode on the spot. For the rest of my middle school days, I was sure that this kid resented me. He held something against me that was completely out of my hands – something that was not my fault – simply because I associated with a possible future criminal.

Fast forwarding, the good news is that John, the bike thief, ended up becoming a preacher. I guess he atoned for all the shit he put me through back in the day.

I tell you that story to show you how guilt by association often plays out. It doesn't just happen with stolen bikes, though. It can be incorporated into our everyday lives. It might even play out with the thoughts we share with other people.

Your thoughts can rub off on those you interact with. If you're someone who is always feeling gloomy, the other people you spend time with will feel it as well. Even generally happy people might catch that gloom. So, keep that in mind when you decide who you want to spend time with.

It's not a coincidence that negative people often have fewer people who want to spend time with them. We have to be careful – not only about the thoughts we put in our heads, but with what we're saying out loud, too. I often say, "If you wanna think negative thoughts, keep them to yourself, don't spew them onto me!"

That being said, I am not a saint, nor do I always do things right. I'm sure I can be negative from time to time. However, I do quickly try to correct myself if I am being negative. I do this because I know it's not just myself that I have an effect on, but other folks as well. I don't want to make them guilty of being negative... by association.

Whether you know it or not, you have a way to positively or negatively affect everyone around you. The power of our words and actions is one of the strongest things that we have as human beings. One way to use that power is to learn to filter your thoughts. You may think it's harmless to share everything that happens to you. You may think, *what's so bad about telling my coworkers about the fact that I woke up with a headache, then got pulled over and spilled coffee all over myself, making me late for work?* Really think about it, though. Does telling them that story really improve the lives of the people around you... or are you just being selfish?

Don't be guilty by associating with those who think, speak, and act negatively. To make sure you're not guilty of that, I challenge you to reflect on your day. Do you have a lot of negative thoughts? Do you feel like you are sharing those negative thoughts a lot? If so, then maybe it's time to think about a different approach. Maybe you can put a positive spin on your day, rather than a negative one. Sure, that's going to be hard. Yes, we all need to vent. But don't make that venting an everyday action. Always venting will just flood the ducts with negativity. Too much venting could result in you losing friends, not to mention the adverse effects of filling your brain with negativity. So, do your best to find the positivity in every situation.

# CHAPTER 20:

# IT IS YOUR RESPONSIBILITY

Unfortunately, the word "responsible" gets thrown around way too much in our world. It often has a negative connotation, especially from when we were kids. If something in the house broke, your parents may have asked, "Who is responsible?!" Or, if your parents are going on vacation, they may have lectured you on "being responsible" and not throwing any keg parties. Luckily for my parents, I was pretty damn responsible, but sometimes, I find myself wishing that I had been less responsible growing up. It seemed like the less responsible kids had more fun, but that may have only just been in the moment. More likely than not, those fun (but poor) decisions ended up not working out in the long run.

You will always have some sort of responsibility. One of the most prevalent, and important, is the idea of taking responsibility for your thoughts and actions. Many great philosophers have said that their lives started to improve once they started taking responsibility for everything. At times, this responsibility was extremely daunting and difficult. It's important, though. Take responsibility for everything, even the negative things. If you get stuck on the train tracks on your way to work, making you late and resulting in your car getting totaled, that's your responsibility. It's not your fault that there was a train. Sure, you're not the conductor, and you also don't make the train schedules. But you are the conductor and scheduler of your own life. When you start taking responsibility for your life, you might just find that things will get easier. Not only that, but people might even want to be around you more. Some may even think that you have some kind of special skill.

As humans it's easy for us to blame things on other people. It might seem innocent at first, but eventually, pointing the finger at outside forces will come back to bite you. By blaming other people, the weather, or your dog that ate your homework, you are taking the easy way out. It starts with something simple, then turns into a life of procrastination. Because now – somehow, someway – you can find an excuse. But I guarantee you that some of the most successful people on the planet are not people who just wait around for things to happen. They make it happen.

So, stop blaming others. You probably should have communicated better, or checked the weather report and brought an umbrella, or put your backpack where your dog couldn't reach it.

I had a coworker a few years ago who did not say a lot of smart things, but he did have one wise phrase: "You can take responsibility for all the good things that happen around you, but you also have to take responsibility for all the bad." He said it so much that I'd be surprised if it's not inscribed on his tombstone. He said it for a reason, though. If you were a volleyball coach and your team won a match, it would be easy to pat yourself on the back for a job well-done. If you do that, though, you also need to take responsibility if your team loses. As humans, it's easy to feel better when someone else is responsible for the bad things. Even if you're the greatest at what you do, others will feel better about you if you take responsibility.

# CHAPTER 21:

# DO NOT WAIT FOR THINGS TO HAPPEN

**W**hen I attended summer camp in fifth grade, I received a postcard from my mom and dad. I do not know why, but I remember the card to this day. I can still see the green background behind the man riding a bike up a mountain. It read "Do not wait for things to happen, Go out and happen to things."

At the time, I did not really think much about the card. I was probably too busy going down the water slide and eating s'mores. But I held onto that postcard, keeping it in my drawer for years. I may have not fully understood the message at 12 years old, but as I grew up, I discovered that it is one hundred percent true. Sometimes, we hear people talk about things they want to do, saying, "I'm just waiting for the right time." Many times, "someday" is just a synonym for "never." That may not always be the case, but it's often used as an excuse to put off something. If you tell your spouse that you'll take out the trash "one of these day," or that you'll do the dishes "eventually," you might as well be asking *them* to do it instead...

The truth is, in order to get anything done, you must take action. If you ask most people their regrets, I would bet that most of those would be about things they didn't do, rather than what they did. So, act. Act so that you don't have those regrets. There will be risk involved with anything you do. It is important to understand your level of risk. Be aware of it, analyze it, and to know all you are in for. But, don't let the risk of falling come with never climbing.

Great things in life sometimes do not come without taking the leap. There never will be a "perfect time" to take risk. The time is when you are emotionally ready and have the proper mindset for the journey. Whether it be training for a marathon or starting your own business, You will never know what to expect, so just get ready and expect the unexpected. Some say "Good things come to those who wait", I say "Good things come to those who take chances and hustle! Don't wait for things to happen, Go out and happen to things.

# CHAPTER 22:

## YOU ARE NOT YOUR PAST

believe that in life, age comes with knowledge.

The challenge is that some people spend most of their lives trying to figure out the past. They rely on that to help them succeed. But all of that – where you were born, your education (or lack thereof), and your rich (or nonexistent) parents – doesn't matter! The past can be a great teacher, sure, but it also can be our worst enemy.

A lot of people say, "I can't be _____ because my parents _____." Fill in those blanks yourself.

"I will never be <u>rich</u> because my parents and grandparents were <u>poor</u>."

"I can't <u>go to college</u> because my parents <u>never did</u>."

Now, that's not to say that these things aren't important. They have shaped who you and your family are. But you can't let it block you. You are your own future.

You might find yourself using these excuses for thirty years and spend those thirty years basking in the decisions caused by those excuses. However, remember that your past doesn't shape you. People often forget this, but it's okay to start over. So, don't spend all that time regretting choices you made and the people you met. Don't let that consume who you are.

I have a friend, who I will call Jessica. She dated this guy in college named Jack, and she was sure that she loved him. They were going to be together forever, have three kids (two girls and one boy) and a dog named Spot. She only dated this guy for six months, but he was, apparently, "the one." Her parents, however, were not fans. Shocker. But that only made her want him more. Jack, unfortunately, had terrible credit, so Jessica co-signed on his car. Jack was also always late for his job at Outback, so he made crappy tips and always had to borrow money.

One day, Jessica was going to Panama City Beach on a girls trip, so she spent the night at her girlfriend Amy's house because they planned to get up early the next day. When she awoke, Jessica couldn't resist seeing Jack one last time before takeoff. Romantic, right? So, she made Amy drive her home real quick so she could crawl into bed and give Jack a surprise goodbye kiss. Well, some of you may have a guess as to where this story is going. But if you guessed that he was in bed with another woman, you'd be wrong. He was in bed with *two* other women!

Jessica was so shocked and mortified that she said nothing and left. She couldn't even tell Amy what happened out of pure disbelief and embarrassment. But she eventually broke it off with Jack, and she went on to fail all her classes at college, coming close to dropping out. Eventually, though, she pulled herself together and graduated after five-and-a-half years.

After college, Jessica blamed everything on that six-month run with Jack. He was the reason she was always so emotional, always getting screwed over by guys. She was afraid to love again because she was a product of such an unfortunate situation. On her 30th birthday, after not being able to find a boyfriend, she joined Match.com. It took her a year to realize that it wouldn't work with anyone because of the damage her relationship with Jack had inflicted on her.

People like Jessica take half a lifetime to figure themselves out, spending their adult lives blaming other people and other things on their good or bad existences. When I met Jessica as a co-worker a few years ago, I heard her story for the first time. After listening, I gave her my point of view, which was that she needed to regroup, recharge, and restart. I told her it was okay to not have everything figured out. Just because something bad happens to you, even something life-altering, YOU CAN STILL CHANGE. You are not your past. You are your future – and your future is not determined.

During the first thirty years of our lives, for the most part, everything seems to go by very fast. We face ever-changing circumstances during this time. Over the next thirty years, though, we often find ourselves looking back on these first thirty years, wishing we would have done things differently. But wishing we could change something only makes us feel bad about the decisions we *have* made. As you have learned in this book, you cannot go back and change the past. You can only change *right now*. Some may be harder to change than others, but you have the power.

# CHAPTER 23:

# LET'S PUT A SMILE ON THAT FACE

We all know that life has a way of picking us up, only to knock us down. It's not fun. But one of the most pivotal parts of success and happiness is using humor to protect yourself and others. I didn't have it easy from a young age. I was overweight and had a speech impediment up until high school, but I used humor. Not only was it a defense mechanism, but it made people laugh. Ultimately, I think people liked me more because I was a "funny guy."

I carried what I learned about humor throughout my years. I made people laugh, but tried to look at a different side of life when something crazy happened. I always kept a sense of humor close. The reason was because there was always a lot more in the world that could make me angry than could make me laugh. I'm sure everyone could say the same about themselves.

So, I try to find humor in many situations I find myself in – even the bad ones. This doesn't mean I'm laughing at everything that happens, but I do try to approach everything with humility. Once I stop taking things too seriously, I'm able to find the humor.

Here's an example, and it might work for you: imagine you get a flat tire. Yes, I'm sure you'd be very pissed off. But that doesn't mean you can't laugh. If you were on a plane and were about to take off, but they kept prolonging it, this would probably be incredibly irritating. Doesn't mean you can't make a joke, though. Each of these examples has something you might not realize. If you have a flat tire, you still have a car that works. If you are on a plane, then it means you have the fortune to travel, possibly even on vacation. If you can afford to travel, it means you might just have a job that pays you well. So, if you find yourself upset, ask yourself: is there really something to be that upset about?

Of course, we are humans, and there are things that irritate us every day. But it is a scientific fact that putting a smile on your face or hearing the sound of laughter can actually improve your mood, whatever situation you're in. This includes in a workplace environment. If you are at work, it might be as simple as getting a calendar that tells you a joke a day. There are even apps you can download that will give you a daily joke.

And as crazy as it sounds, sometimes if you are sad or in a bad mood, your way out of that mood could be to just smile. Now, this doesn't mean you have to be creepy and walk around smiling everywhere you go, because that could come across as weird. You might not get many friends that way.

Just kidding.

See. Made you smile!

Some of you may read this and say, "Josh, I recently lost someone special to me," or, "I just lost my job, or, "My dog died recently," so, "Josh, tell me how in the hell I'm supposed to be laughing." To that I would say, one, I am sorry, but two, all of those things are out of your control. But guess what is in your control? Moving your face. So, smile, and know that it can only get better.

There are some people who think that laughing at a situation can be cruel, or that it's not the right thing to do, or that it makes them a bad person. As long as you're not doing it with ill intent, or directly at someone, or making fun of another person's misfortune, though, who cares?

Sometimes, you can laugh together. Because there is a difference between laughing at someone and laughing with someone.

We are all in this life together. No one gets out alive. So,
just try to be nice to people. Tell a joke every once in a while.
Sometimes, you may even be the joke, so try not to take it personally. Because if you're the joke, you might be making someone
else's day brighter. So, laugh together.

Put a smile on someone's face. Before you do that, though,
put a smile on your own face. I've never really met a clown I did
not like – even the Joker from Batman (except for the terrorizing
and killing people, of course). Most of life is funny, even when
it's not.

So, put a smile on that face, and you might just make the
world a little bit brighter.

# CONCLUSION

In closing, if everything in this book were easy, then everybody would have done it already. Changing a long mindset pattern is difficult. However, you have the power to help turn your emotional and physiological mindset any way you want. We truly do not know the time we have left here on Earth. So, start acting right, giving your best, and helping others… even the ones you don't agree with. I'm serious, even them. We are all on this same rock together, passing by each other every day. A few more extra smiles may just go a long way.

Thank you, and have a wonderful day!